LEGENDS OF WARFARE

GROUND

Ford M8 and M20

The US Army's Standard Armored Car of WWII

DAVID DOYLE

SCHIFFER MILITARY

4880 Lower Valley Road   Atglen, PA 19310

Designed by Justin Watkinson
Type set in Impact/Minion Pro/Univers LT Std

ISBN: 978-0-7643-6143-2
Printed in China

Published by Schiffer Publishing, Ltd.
4880 Lower Valley Road
Atglen, PA 19310
Phone: (610) 593-1777; Fax: (610) 593-2002
E-mail: Info@schifferbooks.com
www.schifferbooks.com

For our complete selection of fine books on this and related subjects, please visit our website at www.schifferbooks.com. You may also write for a free catalog.

Schiffer Publishing's titles are available at special discounts for bulk purchases for sales promotions or premiums. Special editions, including personalized covers, corporate imprints, and excerpts, can be created in large quantities for special needs. For more information, contact the publisher.

We are always looking for people to write books on new and related subjects. If you have an idea for a book, please contact us at proposals@schifferbooks.com.

Acknowledgments

This book would not have been possible without the gracious help of many individuals and institutions. Beyond the invaluable help provided by the staffs of the Benson Ford Archives, the TACOM LCMC History Office, the National Archives, and the Patton Museum, I am deeply indebted to Tom Kailbourn, Scott Taylor, the late Richard Hunnicutt, Brent Mullins, Chris Benedict, the late Fred Ropkey, Dana Bell, Bill Kish, Jim Gilmore, Joe DeMarco, Paul Viens, and John Cliche. Their generous and skillful assistance adds immensely to the quality of this volume. In addition to such wonderful friends and colleagues, the Lord has blessed me with a wonderful wife, Denise, who has tirelessly scanned hundreds of photos and documents for this and numerous other books. Beyond that, she is an ongoing source of support and inspiration.

Contents

Introduction

The Ford M8 and M20 armored cars were the US Army's standard armored cars of World War II and for several years later. Making this somewhat remarkable is that these vehicles were developed rather hastily.

Development of these vehicles began in July 1941.

Because at that time the 37 mm Gun M6 was considered an effective antitank gun, the development of the armored car was of interest to the Tank Destroyer Command. Looking ahead, the Army desired that the basic vehicle be adaptable to other roles as well, such as mortar carrier, multiple gun motor carriage, or cargo carrier. Basic military characteristics of such a vehicle were laid down.

Ordnance Committee Minutes (OCM) of October 9, 1941, recommended that two pilot 37 mm gun motor carriages, one each from Ford and the Fargo Division of Chrysler Corporation, be procured. These vehicles were to be designated T22 and T23. This recommendation was approved by OCM 17359 on October 22.

However, this decision was revised by OCM 17515 of December 10, 1941, which upped the recommendation to two pilots from each manufacturer.

The four vehicles were to be in the following configurations:

6×6	Ford	37 mm Gun Motor Carriage T22
4×4	Ford	37 mm Gun Motor Carriage T22E1
6×6	Fargo	37 mm Gun Motor Carriage T23
4×4	Fargo	37 mm Gun Motor Carriage T23E1

Shortly thereafter, the Studebaker Corporation of South Bend, Indiana, offered to build a similar vehicle, for test by the government, at its own expense. This vehicle, while encompassing the military characteristics set forth for the T22 series, would feature independent suspension.

On January 29, 1942, the government accepted this offer through OCM 17718 and designated the Studebaker vehicle as the 37 mm Gun Motor Carriage T43.

That designation was short lived, since on March 12, 1942, per OCM 17929, all the vehicles were redesignated as follows:

37 mm Gun Motor Carriage T22 becomes
Light Armored Car T22
37 mm Gun Motor Carriage T22E1 becomes
Light Armored Car T22E1
37 mm Gun Motor Carriage T23 becomes
Light Armored Car T23
37 mm Gun Motor Carriage T23E1 becomes
Light Armored Car T23E1
37 mm Gun Motor Carriage T43 becomes
Light Armored Car T21

Six days prior, the vehicles had received a more substantive change when OCM 17906 recommended eliminating the bow machine gun and specified the armament to be one 37 mm M6 cannon and one M1919A4 .30-caliber machine gun mounted coaxially in a Combination Mount M23 installed in the turret. Four M1928A1 Thompson .45-caliber submachine guns would be provided for the crew.

The Ford pilot began testing on the company grounds at Dearborn, Michigan, on March 5, 1942, and was dispatched to Aberdeen Proving Ground in Maryland for testing on March 12. It was displayed at an Ordnance demonstration there on March 16 and the next day was driven by representatives of the Armored Force. At the request of the commanding general of the Armored Force, arrangements were made to drive the vehicle to Fort Knox on March 19 for testing there. The vehicle arrived at Fort Knox

The US Army's Ordnance Department issued a requirement in July 1941 for two pilots of a light, low-silhouette, self-propelled, 6×6 wheeled gun carriage, armed with a 37 mm antitank gun and .30-caliber coaxial machine gun, but also adaptable to other combinations of weapons or conversion to a cargo carrier. Development of the two pilots was authorized three months later; Ford Motor Company produced a 37 mm Gun Motor Carriage T22, while the Fargo Motor Corporation Subsidiary of Chrysler Corporation built a 37 mm Gun Motor Carriage T23. Just after the United States entered World War II, the requirement was expanded to include two additional, 4×4 pilots: the Ford 37 mm Gun Motor Carriage T22E1 and the Fargo T23E1. The T22, shown here, featured a raised armored shield over the drivers' compartment, a round turret with tapered sides, prominent fenders, and a large, sloped glacis with a .30-caliber bow machine gun on the right side. *Patton Museum*

on March 20, and three days of testing began the next day. At the conclusion of these tests, the Armored Force was impressed with the vehicle and felt that with some modifications, it was suitable for standardization as a reconnaissance vehicle by the Armored Force and Cavalry. The Tank Destroyer Command felt it met the requirements for a 37 mm gun motor carriage as well. While the conventional chassis design limited the cross-country speed of the vehicle, it also meant that the vehicle should be able to be placed in mass production quickly.

The modifications that were requested were the following:

- provision for a .50-caliber antiaircraft weapon at the rear of the turret
- use of a 12-volt electrical system in lieu of the 6-volt system of the pilot
- inclusion of an auxiliary generator to maintain battery charge for radio use without running the vehicle main engine
- bullet splash protection for the driver and assistant driver
- provision of periscopes for the driver and assistant driver

The Armored Force, Cavalry, and Tank Destroyer Command indicated a need for 3,534 of the vehicles, with 1,534 of them going to the Tank Destroyers.

Because of the positive reception to the T22, on April 23, 1942, OCM 18133 approved the termination of the T22E1, T23, and T23E1 projects. The pilots then under construction would be completed, and the resultant vehicles would be used for testing.

The Studebaker T21 was delivered to the General Motors Proving Ground, a government contractor, for testing on May 22. Testing there revealed that the ratios between fourth and fifth gears were too close together, and second and third too far apart. There were also a couple of clutch failures, which were attributed to overspeeding, and the layout of the driver's compartment made it uncomfortable for a tall driver. Following tests by the Special Armored Vehicle Board in October–November 1942, it was recommended that development of this vehicle too be terminated, which was done on January 21, 1943, per OCM 19543.

On May 19, 1942, OCM 18314 recommended the standardization of the modified T22 as the Light Armored Car M8. This was approved on June 25, 1942, by OCM 18390. Five days prior to this, the British Tank Mission advised the US Tank Committee that the United Kingdom had no requirement for the vehicles.

On July 15, 1942, OCM 18511 specified that in view of the light armor of the M8, all such vehicles shipped overseas were to be equipped with self-sealing fuel tanks.

On March 12, the designation of the 37 mm Gun Motor Carriage T22 was changed to Light Armored Car T22. This photo of the vehicle was taken six days later, on March 18, 1942, during testing at Aberdeen Proving Ground, Maryland. Details in view include the service headlights with blackout lamps above them, all without brush guards; the bow machine gun mount; and the horn on the right fender. Two tow eyes and shackles are on the bottom frontal plate of the vehicle. The vision slits on the drivers'-compartment armored flaps are arranged in sets of four, with two upper and two lower slits. A storage box is mounted between the front and center wheels. *Chris Benedict collection*

This is the Ford 37 mm Gun Motor Carriage T22E1, which Ford designated its Model GAM. Both the T22 and the T22E1 included provisions for a ball mount for a .30-caliber machine gun on the right side of the glacis, a feature that did not carry over to production M8s. *Patton Museum*

In an original color photograph, the Ford T22E1 is poised above a pond at a testing ground. At this time, no fenders were installed. The panels of the armored shield for the drivers' compartment were hinged, and they are lowered in this photo. The turret lacks the 37 mm gun mount. *Vintage Power Wagons collection*

In a photo likely taken on the same occasion as the preceding one, the Ford T22E1 is splashing through a shallow pond at a testing ground. Note the folded-down frontal shield of the drivers' compartment, and the rather tall brush guards for the headlights on the glacis. On the bank in the background is a six-wheeled 37 mm gun motor carriage that appears to be the Fargo T23. *Vintage Power Wagons collection*

The Fargo Division of Chrysler produced one pilot T23 in response to the Army's July 1941 requirement for a six-wheeled 37 mm gun motor carriage. The design of the T23 varied in several respects from that of the Ford T22, having a longer glacis with no bow machine gun, a trapezoidal gun shield on the front of the cast turret, sponsons that extended over the wheels in lieu of fenders, and a sponson between the front and center wheels. *Vintage Power Wagons collection*

In addition to the four 37 mm gun motor carriage pilots submitted by Ford and Fargo, the Studebaker Corporation, on its own initiative, produced one pilot vehicle for consideration by the Army: the six-wheeled 37 mm Gun Motor Carriage T43. This vehicle was redesignated the Light Armored Car T21 on March 12, 1942. It featured a stepped bow instead of the pronounced glacises of the Ford and Fargo armored cars, and a prominent sponson was between the front and center wheels. *TACOM LCMC History Office*

The Studebaker Light Armored Car T21 was photographed during trials at Aberdeen Proving Ground on November 16, 1942. The T21 had the same military characteristics as the M22 and had the added benefit of independent suspensions, which the M22 and, later, the M8 lacked. *Patton Museum*

The rear of the Studebaker T21 was equipped with louvers. On the side of the rear of the vehicle is the muffler. A tow pintle is visible on the rear cross-member of the chassis.

Details on the upper part of the T21 are displayed. Ventilation ports are on the engine cover, which has two sections, each with two hinges on the front end. The turret was of cast steel. The drivers' armored shields are lowered, showing the insides of the direct-vision ports. *Patton Museum*

CHAPTER 1
The M8

On July 23, 1942, the letter purchase order was received by Ford for facilities, machinery, and equipment only, to produce 6,000 M8 armored cars and sixty sets of spare parts at a rate of 1,250 per month. Supplement number 1, issued the same day, was for the 6,000 vehicles and parts themselves. The contract number was W-374-ORD-1744. Four days later, an additional supplement to this order arrived, calling for a further 5,070 M8s and fifty-one sets of spare parts. Only two days later, Ford began converting their Chicago plant to produce these vehicles, which were assigned Ford model numbers GAK. On August 12, 1942, a formal supplement was issued to contract W-374-ORD-1744, reducing the number of vehicles to 8,460 at a rate of 1,500 per month. At that time, plans were in place to produce the vehicles at Ford facilities in Chicago and Kansas City.

However, these were not the first armored cars that Ford had been contracted to build during World War II. That honor had gone to the Heavy Armored Car T17, which was produced at the Ford Twin Cities plant. Development of this heavy armored car had begun only a few months earlier. That project culminated in two vehicles, the Ford T17 Deerhound and the Chevrolet T17E1 Staghound. The latter was produced exclusively for the British Empire and was built in the thousands, seeing wide use. The former was also produced for the British, but the Commonwealth never took delivery of them. Instead, the US Army accepted the truncated production run of 250 vehicles.

This decision would free the Twin Cities plant for M8 production, plus the plant was already set up for armored-car production. Thus, the plan to build armored cars in Kansas City was abandoned, and the Twin Cities plant converted accordingly.

Production of the M8 got underway at both Chicago and the Twin Cities in March 1943, with three vehicles being produced in the former, and a dozen in the latter.

Despite the ambitious production schedule for these vehicles that initially was called for, the war priority rating given to the vehicles was such that those rates could never be attained. Rather, the high was in September 1943, when the Twin Cities plant turned out 572 of the vehicles. Twin Cities equaled that number again in December 1943, but production through 1943 averaged about 150 M8s per month. Chicago reached its peak in October 1943, at 200 of the vehicles.

On December 7, 1944, OCM 25967 recommended that the M8 be reclassified as Substitute Standard. This recommendation was approved on March 1, 1945. On October 11, 1945, it was recommended that this change again, to Limited Standard, and this was approved on November 15.

Production of the M8 ceased in May 1945, except for spare parts. At that time, the Twin Cities plant had built 6,397 M8 vehicles and Chicago had built 2,127 such machines. The contract was completely terminated on August 17, 1945.

In May 1942, the Army tendered Ford an order for 5,000 production light armored cars, an improved version of the T22 designated the T22E2 and later standardized as the M8. Contractual problems caused a delay in the start of production until March 1943. As seen in this photo of an early T22E2, these vehicles incorporated many revisions over Ford's T22, including a redesigned engine deck, capacious fenders, the omission of the bow machine gun, and redesigned armor for the drivers, which incorporated a fixed armored hood with hinged top and front covers. The top covers opened to the sides, while the front covers swung down flat on the glacis. At this point in its development, the M8 lacked the supports for the drivers' top hatch covers on the sides of the drivers' hood.

This vehicle evidently was a preproduction Light Armored Car T22E2, shown during testing at Aberdeen Proving Ground on November 16, 1942, four months before series production of the T22E2/M8 commenced. Two antiaircraft machine guns were mounted on the cast-steel turret for testing. On a pedestal on the rear of the turret was a Browning M1919A4 .30-caliber machine gun, while a Browning M2 HB .50-caliber machine gun was on a pedestal on the turret roof. The registration number of this vehicle, W-6038230, is puzzling, since the Ordnance Department's May 1, 1945, list of armored, tank, and combat vehicles indicates that this registration number equates to a serial number in the 6000 range, whereas it is known that the first T22E2 was serial number 6. *Patton Museum*

The T22E2 and M8 featured a large panel with louvers on the rear of the hull. Jutting from the upper part of the rear of the hull were two taillight assemblies, above which were lifting rings. Storage boxes called "fender boxes" were incorporated into the hull above the rear wheels, and their hinged lids are visible: a narrow one with one lock hasp, *to the front*, and a longer one with two hasps, *to the rear*. At three places on the turret exterior are groups of four slotted screws: two groups on the left side of the turret and one on the right side. These were for securing the seat support bracket: the frame that held the gunner's and commander's seats and the firing pedals for the 37 mm and .30-caliber weapons. *Patton Museum*

The engine deck of the T22E2 / M8 was considerably different from that of the T22, featuring two armored ventilation hoods, positioned over two engine-access doors. On the small roof of the cast turret were periscopes on rotating mounts for the gunner, *left*, and the vehicle commander, *right*. *National Archives*

All but the last digit of the registration number of this T22E2 is visible, and this vehicle is likely the same one shown in the preceding several photos, W-6038230. Here, its turret is shorn of the machine gun pedestals. The photo was taken on August 18, 1942, during evaluations by the Ordnance Operation, General Motors Proving Ground. *Patton Museum*

Several changes were made to the T22E2 / M8 turret around the end of 1942, as seen in this photo of a vehicle with two radio antennas on the right sponson. Because the turret roof interfered with the full operation of the gunner's telescopic sight, the roof was reduced in size and the periscopes were deleted. Rails were installed midway up the turret, and footman loops were applied, for strapping on four blanket rolls, a tarpaulin, and camouflage netting. Another change was the addition of two racks toward the bottom of each sponson for holding three M1A1 antitank mines. Crews also were instructed to use these racks as steps for mounting the vehicle. Supports for the drivers' top hatch covers have been added to the sides of the drivers' hood. *Patton Museum*

A very early-production Light Armored Car M8, registration number 6032232 and serial number 8, was photographed on April 22, 1943. A siren and two combination service headlight–blackout lamp assemblies are installed behind brush guards. On the outboard side of each brush guard is a holder for a plug for the headlight-mounting socket when the headlight is dismounted. On each forward door of the drivers' compartment is a direct-vision port (outboard) and a periscope (inboard). Jutting from the side of the drivers' compartment hood is a holder for the top door when open. *TACOM LCMC History Office*

A turret assembly is suspended from a sling above the hull of a very early Light Armored Car M8, registration number 6032230, serial number 6. Faintly visible on the side of the turret are decals giving the storage locations of blanket rolls and tarpaulin. Suspended from the turret is a tripod frame supporting the seats and the firing pedals for the guns. The slotted screws sometimes seen on the exteriors of early turrets, for attaching the frame, are not present. *Benson Ford Archives*

In a companion view to the preceding photo, the turret is just inches above the hull of M8 registration number 6032230. Vendors supplied the turrets and turret rings for the M8s to Ford. Despite some sources' insistence that the turrets for the Light Armored Car M8 were of welded construction, in fact only a single turret was of welded, or fabricated, construction, and it was used solely for researching the production problems such a turret would entail. Turrets arrived at Ford's plants as rough castings. After being inspected, they were machined in Betts boring machines. Subsequently, radial drills and special machines were used to perform necessary drilling and embossing operations on the turrets. Defects in the turret surfaces were repaired by welding. *Benson Ford Archives*

During the early development of the M8, experiments were made with several types of mounts for antiaircraft machine guns. This photo depicts a Browning M2 HB .50-caliber machine gun on the D67511 folding pintle mount, as installed on M8 registration number 6032258. This type of mount began appearing on production M8s by the summer of 1944. Note the travel lock for the .50-caliber machine gun on the turret roof, and the presence of detachable windshields for the drivers. Development of these windshields for M8s began around early July 1943. They were made of safety glass in a metal frame with rubber molding and a windshield wiper. *Benson Ford Archives*

The .50-caliber antiaircraft machine gun on Light Armored Car M8 with registration number 6032250 is shown stored for travel atop the turret. Another photo of this vehicle taken on or around the same occasion depicts the machine gun on a D67511 folding pintle mount. Camouflage in the form of light-colored squiggles has been painted on the vehicle. *TACOM LCMC History Office*

This photo and the following six images were taken by the Ordnance Department for the reference of the Tank Destroyer Board; they show the first production Light Armored Car M8 with, according to the cover letter dated March 24, 1943, "all stowage in place." The on-vehicle equipment includes a snap-on canvas cover over the turret, blanket rolls and a rolled tarpaulin on the turret, a shovel, and even antitank mines in canvas covers on the rack along the sponson. *Patton Museum*

A close-up view of the first production M8 provides details of the snap-on canvas cover for the turret. An ax is stored next to the shovel. To the front of the turret, and behind the drivers' hood, is an M5A1 cleaning staff, for the 37 mm gun. Below the front blanket roll, note the four countersunk, slotted screws, which are attached to the seat support bracket: the frame supporting the seats and the firing pedals in the turret. *Patton Museum*

A view of the right side of the first production M8 illustrates how the blanket rolls and tarpaulin roll are secured with straps through the footman loops and around the rail on the side of the turret. Decals mark the storage locations of the mattock handle and the antitank mines. The L-shaped object on the codriver's top door is a swiveling handle. Handles are permanently welded to the front doors of the drivers' compartment. *Patton Museum*

The interior of the turret of the same M8 is seen from the right side of the turret. The commander's seat, *foreground*, and the gunner's seat are mounted on the white-colored seat support bracket. On the turret wall between the seats is a storage rack for eight rounds of 37 mm ammunition. On the white ring around the base of the turret is an azimuth scale, officially called the index plate. The white handwheel is for traversing the turret; this was the wheel used with the early-type, one-speed traversing mechanism. An M1 carbine is stored on each rear post of the seat support bracket. *Patton Museum*

The interior of the same turret is viewed from the rear. To the left of the 37 mm gun breech is the gunner's telescopic sight and head guard. To the right of the 37 mm breech are the Browning M1919A4 .30-caliber coaxial machine gun, a holder for binoculars, and eight rounds of 37 mm ready ammunition. Above the gun breech are the guide track for coaxial machine-gun ammunition, and a compass. *Patton Museum*

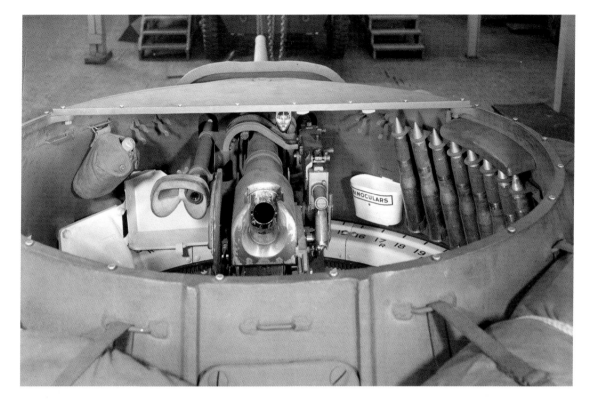

In a view down into the turret of the first production M8, snaps for securing a canvas cover on the turret are around the top edge of the turret. Details of the recoil guard of the 37 mm gun are available. Attached to the guard is a canvas collector bag for spent casings. The sides of the interior of the hull are painted white, while the floor is Olive Drab. On the right side of the hull are sliding doors for the 37 mm ammunition compartment located in the right sponson. On the left side of the hull, below the traversing handwheel, in the left sponson, is a radio rack, below which is storage space for machine gun ammunition. *Patton Museum*

In this photo looking down into the turret of the M8, the turret roof is to the lower right, and the top of the 37 mm gun breech is at the center. The relative locations of the two ready racks for 37 mm ammunition are apparent: they are on the rear and the right side of the turret, within reach of the vehicle commander, who also served as the loader. *Patton Museum*

In the first of a series of photos dated February 25, 1944, Light Armored Car M8 with registration number 6035164 and serial number 2940 is viewed from the right front. Note how a webbing strap attached to footman loops serves to hold in place the three M1A1 antitank mines. *Patton Museum*

Light Armored Car M8 with registration number 6035164 is observed from the right rear. Snap hooks on retainer chains serve to hold shut the lids of the fender boxes. A roll of camouflage netting is strapped to the rear of the turret, and a heavy-duty tow pintle is on the rear of the chassis frame. *Patton Museum*

In a left-front view of M8 registration number 6035164, a canvas cover is fitted over the 37 mm gun, the .30-caliber coaxial machine gun, and the gun shield. *Patton Museum*

The same M8 is seen from the left side, with the 37 mm gun slightly elevated. The gun had a range of elevation from +20 degrees to –10 degrees. A stencil on the hinged skirt for the rear wheels indicates that two radio sets were installed: an SCR-506 and an SCR-508. *Patton Museum*

On the glacis of the M8 are welded, laterally, two strips of steel, one below and one above the headlight assemblies. These were splash guards, to deflect ricocheting bullet fragments. The object on the glacis above the top of the star contains hold-down latches for the drivers' front hatch covers. *Patton Museum*

On the rear of the hull of M8 registration number 6035164 are armored louvers, to protect the radiator to the immediate front of the louvers. Note the tilted positioning of the tow eyes and clevises below the louvers. On the engine-compartment doors are armored ventilation hoods. *Patton Museum*

Light Armored Car M8 with registration number 6035164 is equipped with blanket rolls, a camouflage net on the rear of the turret, and a rolled tarpaulin that wraps around the sides and the rear of the turret. One section of radio antenna is attached to each of the two antenna base units to the rear of the turret. *Patton Museum*

The general arrangement of the top of the M8, as well as the placement of the blanket rolls and camouflage net on the turret, is displayed in this overhead photo of registration number 6035164 on February 25, 1944. Note the recesses in the tops of the engine-compartment doors, above which the ventilation hoods are positioned. The feature spanning the hull to the rear of the turret is the fuel tank cover, on the right end of which is a hinged panel for accessing the fuel filler. *Patton Museum*

The right engine-compartment door of M8 registration number 6035164 is open, permitting a partial view of the Hercules JXD engine. In the right foreground is the 12-volt storage battery. To the left is the radiator. Between the battery and the radiator is the generator. Below the generator is the distributor, made by Electric Auto-Lite. *Patton Museum*

The left engine-compartment door is open, showing the carburetor air cleaner, *left*, with the carburetor air inlet attached to the rear of the air cleaner and the air inlet tube and the carburetor on the inboard side of the air cleaner. Fan belts and radiator are to the right. To the far left is the fuel tank, painted white. *Patton Museum*

The driver's (*left*) and codriver's (*right*) compartments of M8 registration number 6035164 are viewed from above, with blanket rolls on the turret at the bottom and the open front hatch covers to the top. Inside the driver's hatch are the steering wheel and the instrument panel, with a stored M1 carbine to the left of the instrument panel. In the codriver's compartment, to the front of the hatch, is a compass, with intercom equipment on the right wall. Correspondence of the Engineering-Manufacturing Branch, Tank-Automotive Department, in Detroit, dated September 7, 1943, indicated that brackets for Sherrill compasses were to be installed in this location in M8s "on or before the 1,000th vehicle." The actual Sherrill compasses were not ready at that time and were to be installed when available. Note the bulge in the floor, to provide clearance for the front differential. *Patton Museum*

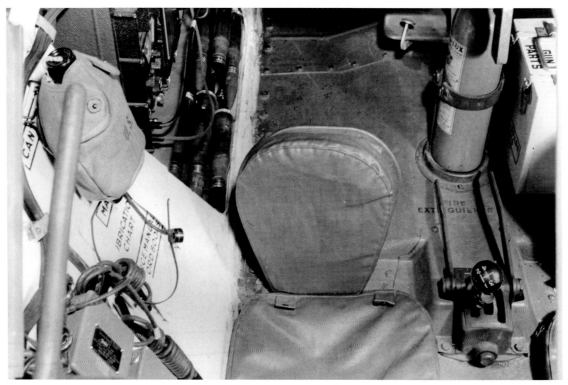

In the right-front seat of the M8 was the codriver (also called assistant driver), who, like the gunner, also functioned as a radio operator. In a view of the codriver's compartment facing the rear, to the left are intercom boxes and a holder for a lubrication chart and vehicle manuals. In the right sponson is a radio, below which are stacked 37 mm rounds. At the center is the codriver's seat, to the side of which are three levers: the center one is the gearshift lever, to the rear of which are, lying close to the floor, the front-axle engaging lever (closest to the seat), and the transfer-case ratio-selecting lever. To the right rear are a fire extinguisher and a case for gun parts. *Patton Museum*

This February 1944 overhead of the driver's position of M8 registration number 6035164 reveals the 5-gallon can stowed behind the driver. In the left sponson can be seen the radio installation, and below that small arms ammunition stowage. *Patton Museum*

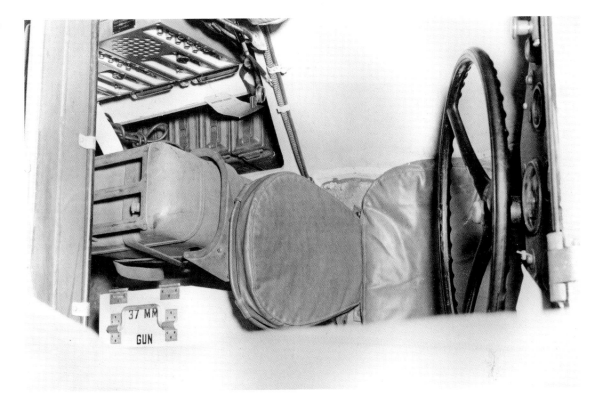

Looking to the front of an M8 along the centerline, the stowage for the protectoscopes and headlamps can be seen. At far left, beyond the steering wheel, the right side of the instrument panel is visible. *Patton Museum*

In response to the continuing need for an antiaircraft machine gun mount on the Light Armored Car M8, the Cavalry Board conducted tests of an M49C ring mount on the turret. Ultimately, by April 1944 the D67511 folding pintle mount was adopted as the standard antiaircraft mount for the M8, but nevertheless, large numbers of M49C ring mounts were installed on these vehicles in the field. Here, an M49C ring mount on an M8, registration number 6032268, is undergoing evaluations at Aberdeen Proving Ground in November 1943. The machine gun is the Browning M2 HB .50-caliber type. *Patton Museum*

An elevated view of the M49C on M8 registration number 6032268 at Aberdeen in November 1943 offers a good view of the circular skate rail, on which the carriage bearing the antiaircraft machine gun and pintle mount traveled as needed, with a traverse of 360 degrees. The ring was mounted on three heavy-duty metal supports, attached to the turret. *Patton Museum*

A surviving Light Armored Car M8 preserved at the US Veterans Memorial Museum in Huntsville, Alabama, is the subject of the following series of photos. It is equipped with an M49C ring mount. This example of mount is installed on three tubular supports. *John Omenski, US Veterans Memorial Museum*

The right side of the engine compartment of the M8 at Huntsville is shown, with the radiator and right fan to the left, the generator to the left of center, and a replacement battery at the lower right. Below the generator is the brown-colored distributor. The black cylinder at the center is the oil filter; to the right is the combination oil-filler cap and crankcase breather. *David Doyle*

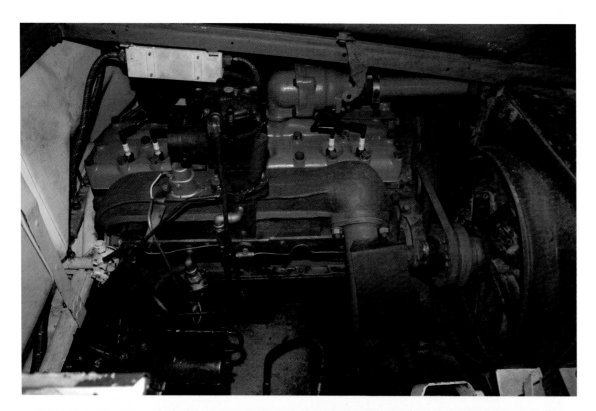

A view inside the left side of the engine compartment reveals the fuel tank, *left*, and the Hercules JXD engine, including the valve cover and spark plugs and the rusted exhaust manifold. On the top of the engine are the radio filter for the distributor (*left*), the carburetor (*center*), and the thermostat housing (*right*). *David Doyle*

The left engine-compartment door of the M8 is open, showing the T-shaped ventilation opening in it; the ventilator hood on the exterior of the door provides protection for the opening. The hold-open rod is connected to a bracket welded to the door. *David Doyle*

Racks for three M1A1 antitank mines are viewed from above; they were fabricated from welded steel. Note the slots on the turn-backs of the upper rack, for attaching webbing straps for securing the mines in place. *David Doyle*

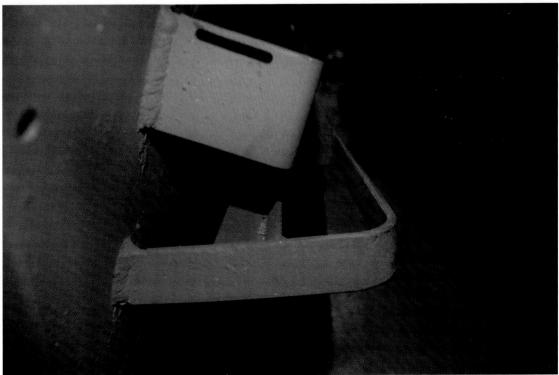

Mine racks are viewed close-up from the side, showing the weld beads and the slot for a strap on the upper rack. *David Doyle*

The turret of the M8 at Huntsville is viewed from the left rear, showing the tubular rear leg of the M49C ring mount and the removable panel on the rear of the turret. This panel is secured with four oval-headed, slotted screws and is bordered on the sides and bottom by a splash shield. *David Doyle*

The method of attaching the ring of the M49C mount to an angle iron welded to the top of one of the tubular supports is illustrated. Details of the Browning M2 HB .50-caliber machine gun and its cradle-and-pintle mount also are shown. The cradle body is part number D58626, and the pintle is the C90812. *David Doyle*

The interior of the turret of the Huntsville M8 includes the 37 mm gun and coaxial M1919A4 .30-caliber coaxial machine gun, along with a partial recoil guard. *David Doyle*

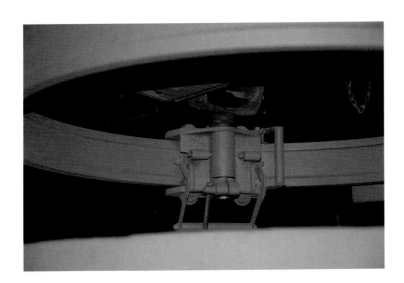

In a view of the M49C ring mount from below, the carriage for the machine gun and its cradle-and-pintle mount is at the center. This carriage incorporated rollers to allow it to move freely around the ring mount. On the bottom of the carriage are the brake lever and the pintle-clamping screw and handle. *David Doyle*

The turret is viewed from the gunner's perspective, with his telescopic sight and head guard to the left, to the right of which are the 37 mm gun, recoil guard, and elevating handwheel. On the opposite wall of the turret is an eight-round rack for 37 mm ammunition. *David Doyle*

After the Ordnance Department ordered the M49C ring mount to be installed on all new-production Light Armored Cars M8 beginning in December 1943, the department reversed its decision in the spring of 1944, instead authorizing the installation of the much-lighter and more compact D67511 folding pintle mount. On this mount, the machine gun was pinned to a cradle assembly, which in turn pivoted on a support assembly. The bottom of the support assembly was pinned to a pintle assembly, which fit into a socket incorporated into a plate that was screwed to the rear of the turret. *Benson Ford Archives*

When the gun was trained to the rear, as seen here, the gunner could operate the weapon from inside the turret. Whereas the original removable plate on the rear of the turret was secured with four screws, the plate with the socket used with the D67511 folding pintle mount required three screws on each side, with two upper screws spaced close to each other. *Benson Ford Archives*

When the gunner fired the machine gun on the D67511 folding pintle mount toward the front, it was necessary for him to operate outside the turret. Despite being authorized as the antiaircraft machine gun mount for the M8, the D67511 mount evidently did not see widespread operational use in World War II. Instead, ring mounts are more commonly seen in photographs from that conflict. *Benson Ford Archives*

For travel, the D67511 mount was released from its upright position by removing pins from the cradle and the support and was folded down and secured, complete with machine gun, whose barrel was secured in a travel lock on the turret roof. The folding pintle mount had the benefit of giving the turret better balance, making it much easier to traverse the turret in certain situations. *Benson Ford Archives*

The Light Armored Car M8 in this and the following photos was in the collection of the late Fred Ropkey. It exhibits the later type removable plate with integral mounting for the D67511 folding pintle. All six of the mounting screws are visible from this angle. *David Doyle*

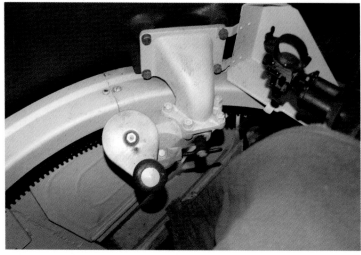

The early type of single-speed turret-traversing mechanism, which had a spoked handwheel, was problematic when tracking slow-moving targets. This photo shows the two-speed traversing mechanism that replaced the one-speed type. The two-speed mechanism featured a teardrop-shaped crank with a knob for a handle. On the handle is a button for shifting between the gears. The T-shaped handle next to the traversing control is the turret lock. The entire assembly is bolted to four bosses on the turret wall. *David Doyle*

This view was taken from the roof of the turret looking down, showing the seats, the canvas cover over the breech of the 37 mm gun, and the two ready racks for 37 mm ammunition. Whereas the seat-bracket assembly in the earliest M8 turrets was attached to the turret by screws whose heads were visible on the exterior of the turret, this method was supplanted by incorporating bosses on the interior of the turret, which were tapped so that the bracket was screwed on from the inside of the turret. *David Doyle*

An overhead view shows the engine-compartment doors, with one ventilation hood, two latching handles, and one grab handle each. To the rear of the doors are two lifting eyes, and to the sides are the hinged covers for the fender storage compartments. *David Doyle*

The 37 mm gun barrel and the driver's compartment are viewed from above the turret. The forward hatch cover has an operating handle that is welded to the cover, while the top hatch cover has a pivoting handle. *David Doyle*

In an overhead view of the codriver's compartment, a detachable windshield is installed in the front. Near the center of the top hatch cover is welded a U-shaped bracket; when opened, this bracket engaged a latch in the recess in the outer end of the hatch-cover support at the upper center of the photo. *David Doyle*

Details of the interior of the driver's front hatch cover are illustrated, including the periscope with a crash pad on the inboard side and a direct-vision port with a swiveling cover on the outboard side. To the left is the hold-open latch assembly for both of the front hatch covers, with button-shaped latch releases on it. These latches also were operable from the inside of the drivers' compartment. *David Doyle*

The interior of the codriver's open front hatch cover, the detachable windshield, and the top hatch cover are viewed from the front. On the front hatch cover are the direct-vision port and its swiveling cover, and the periscope, with its black crash pad. *David Doyle*

Partway through the production of the Light Armored Car M8, the mine racks on the sides of the sponsons were deleted, and storage boxes were mounted on the sponsons. In addition, a storage box for two detachable windows for the driver and the codriver was installed on the glacis; "WINDSHIELDS" is stenciled on the box. These features are present on M8 registration number 6041228 and serial number 8325, as photographed on August 10, 1944, and documented in the following series of photographs taken for the Ordnance Operation, Engineering Standards Vehicle Laboratory, Detroit, Michigan. The boxes on the sponson had an access door with a piano hinge on the top edge, and two latches on the bottom edge. The machine gun, on a folding pintle mount, is in the raised position. *Patton Museum*

The folding pintle mount for the .50-caliber machine gun is in the travel position in this photograph of M8 number 6041228. The box for the windshields is of welded sheet-metal construction. Welded to the lower front of the box are two angled tabs, which are screwed to the glacis. The front end of the cover is secured to the box with three leaf hinges; two latches are on the rear of the cover. *Patton Museum*

The right sponson box of M8 registration number 6041228 is shown with the cover closed. The upper part of the piano hinge for this cover was spot-welded to the hull. Lateral stiffeners were embossed on the sheet metal of the box and cover. *Patton Museum*

The contents of the right sponson box of the same vehicle includes army field rations, inert M1A1 antitank mines, and what appear to be two canisters. *Patton Museum*

A view of M8 registration number 6041228 from the right rear illustrates the new location of the exhaust tailpipe, which protrudes though a hole in the right mudguard. The muffler is positioned laterally below the rear of the chassis frame, and an exhaust line is visible from the muffler, inboard of the rear wheel. By the time this photo was taken, on August 10, 1944, another new modification to the Light Armored Car M8 was the machine gun tripod, stowed on the right fender. A canvas cover is installed over the upper part of the tripod. *Patton Museum*

Light Armored Car M8 with registration number 6041228 is viewed from the right side with equipment mounted, including blanket rolls and rolled tarpaulin. Note how the stamped stiffeners on the lower part of the storage box on the sponson matched the stiffeners on the skirts by the rear wheels. The tires, mounted on 20-inch Firestone combat rims, are size 9.00-20 Goodrich Silvertowns with nondirectional treads. Firestone combat tires also were used on M8s. *Patton Museum*

An overhead view of M8 registration number 6041228, sporting an unusually large recognition star on the engine-compartment doors, depicts the drivers' hatches open and the folding pintle machine-gun mount in the raised position. Four blanket rolls and a rolled camouflage net are strapped to footman loops on the turret. The stored location of the machine gun tripod on the right fender is shown. A close inspection of the photo reveals that the windshield storage box on the glacis has one bolt to hold down its rear, whereas two bolts were used on the front of the box. *Patton Museum*

The same M8 is observed from the left side with the folding pintle mount in the raised position. The blanket rolls and tarpaulin are secured to the turret with a combination of webbing straps and ropes. *Patton Museum*

The position of the storage box for the detachable windshields for the driver and the codriver on the glacis is illustrated. A tow cable is connected to a clevis on the front-right tow eye. A sun shield is over the aperture for the gunner's telescopic sight on the left side of the gun shield. *Patton Museum*

M8 registration number 6041228 is observed from the rear, with a clear view of the embossed stiffeners on the mudguards. The white paint on the ventilation hoods on the engine compartment doors is part of the unusually large recognition star. *Patton Museum*

In a view of the driver's compartment of M8 6041228, on the left sidewall are a canteen, an intercom box, and a flashlight. The instrument panel contained a speedometer (*lower center*), light switches (*upper corners*), ignition switch (*lower right*), and other gauges and switches. *Patton Museum*

Looking into the driver's compartment from the front, in the left foreground is the driver's seat and safety belt, to the rear of which is a box for 37 mm gun parts and a 5-gallon liquid container for water. Next to the container is the radio set, which appears to be an SCR-508 or SCR-608, below which are machine-gun ammunition boxes. *Patton Museum*

The codriver's compartment is viewed from the left rear corner of his hatch. To the left is a compass, secured to the ceiling. On the sidewall are a flashlight; intercom boxes, cables, and hand microphone; a canteen; and clips holding a lubrication chart. The clips also were used for holding technical and field manuals and maps. *Patton Museum*

At the top of this view of the codriver's compartment, an SCR-506 radio is installed in the right sponson, a space originally designed for storing 37 mm ammunition. On the sidewall below the sponson is a door for a small compartment, originally for storing rations. On many M8s with two radios, including this example, this compartment was used for storing 37 mm ammunition. Secured to brackets on that door is a signal-flag set in a canvas case. *Patton Museum*

The SCR-506 radio is seen from another angle from in the turret, with the breech of the 37 mm Gun M6 and the coaxial Browning M1919A4 .30-caliber machine gun to the left. Also visible are eight ready rounds of 37 mm ammunition in clips on the turret; the stenciled azimuth scale, or index plate, around the base of the turret; and a holder for binoculars. *Patton Museum*

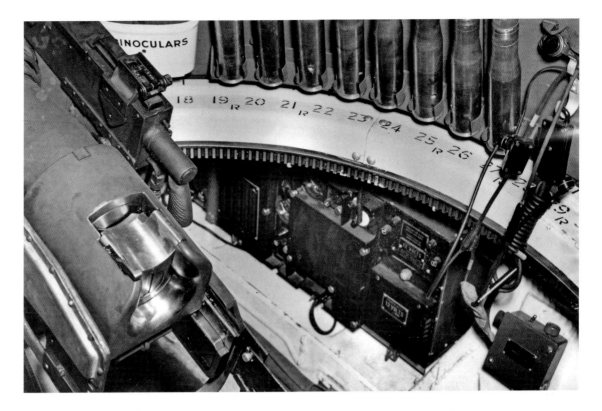

In the turret of M8 registration number 6041228, the two-speed traverse mechanism is to the left, above which is the gunner's telescope and two stored canteens. The breech block of the 37 mm gun operated vertically. Between the breech and the guide track for coaxial machine-gun ammunition are two lugs with holes in them; during travel, these lugs were secured to a lock on the turret roof. To the right is a binocular case in a holder, and several ready rounds of 37 mm ammunition. *Patton Museum*

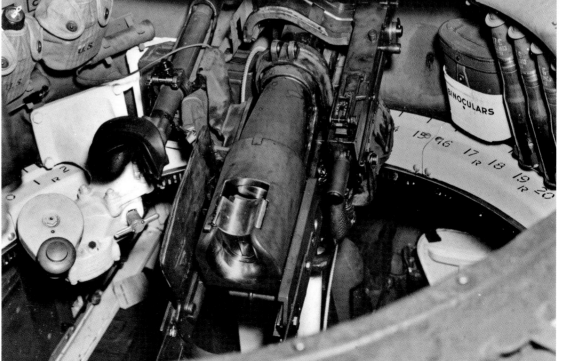

In the turret of M8 registration number 6041228, the two-speed traverse mechanism is to the left, above which is the gunner's telescope and two stored canteens. The breech block of the 37 mm gun operated vertically. Between the breech and the guide track for coaxial machine-gun ammunition are two lugs with holes in them; during travel, these lugs were secured to a lock on the turret roof. *Patton Museum*

In a view into the fighting compartment from the commander/loader's station, part of the radio in the right sponson is visible. Below the radio is a compartment originally designed as a storage space for rations but now used for storing thirty-six rounds of 37 mm ammunition. A dark-colored matting material is on the inner side of the door for this compartment. *Patton Museum*

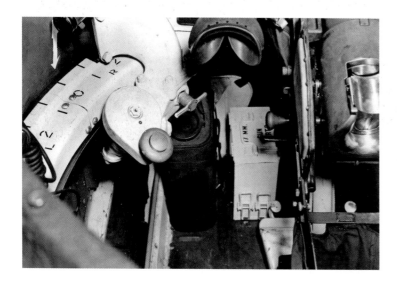

In a gunner's-eye view of the turret interior, the head guard of the telescopic sight is at the upper center, to the left of which are the traversing control and the T-shaped turret-locking handle. Below the gunsight are a 5-gallon container for water and a box for storing spare parts for the 37 mm gun. To the right is the 37 mm gun breech. *Patton Museum*

A photo of the rear of the turret of M8 registration number 6041228 includes details of the seat-support bracket, the ready rack for 37 mm ammunition, and M1 carbines stored on clips on the seat brackets. In the rear of the fighting compartment is a box, lid open, for seven signal flares, flanked by grenade boxes. *Patton Museum*

Because the gunner and the commander of the M8 used the mine racks for steps to climb up to the turret, the new storage boxes on the sides of the sponsons posed a problem in accessing the vehicle. Thus, a step was cut out of the lower-rear part of the boxes. This feature is visible on M8 registration number 60126930. Correspondence of the chief of Ordnance, Washington, DC, dated October 4, 1944, indicated that sponson boxes released for production would have the step incorporated into them. The M8 shown here also is equipped with a .50-caliber machine gun on a folding pintle mount. Several new features are on the rear of the vehicle: the muffler had been moved up from the lower right of the chassis to an opening in the right mudguard, and both mudguards now had embossed stiffeners on them. *Benson Ford Archives*

The Museum of the American GI, in College Station, Texas, preserves this late-type Light Armored Car M8. It is equipped with storage boxes with steps on the sponsons. *David Doyle*

Faintly visible on the upper part of the turret of the M8 at the Museum of the American GI is a raised serial number, 4183. The left headlight is a blackout type, while the right one is a sealed-beam headlight. Both units have blackout marker lamps on top of them. *David Doyle*

A machine gun tripod is stored on the right fender, as was the practice on late M8s. The crew drill manual for the M8 stipulated that the vehicle commander and the gunner mounted the vehicle by using the step on the storage box on the sponson (n early M8s, these crewmen used the mine racks as steps). On the other hand, the driver and the codriver mounted the vehicle from the front. *David Doyle*

The .50-caliber machine gun is installed on a nonfolding pintle mount, secured in the socket on the removable plate on the rear of the turret. On the left mudguard is an armored box containing a first-aid kit, a modification dating to November 1944. *David Doyle*

On the rear cross-member of the chassis frame is a quick-release pintle hook, for towing a trailer. The left taillight assembly has a service brake and taillight with a red-tinted lens, over a blackout taillight, while the right taillight assembly has a blackout brake light over a blackout taillight. *David Doyle*

One of the weaknesses of the Light Armored Car M8 was its nonindependent suspension, which gave the crewmen a rough ride. Also, the front springs were prone to breakage. To address this situation, two M8s were modified with independent front suspensions in September 1943 and were redesignated Light Armored Car M8E1. These front suspensions were of the parallelogram torsion-bar type. While this arrangement made for a much smoother ride, these suspensions were prone to breakdowns. Hence, this project was discontinued at the end of World War II. The smudged registration number on this M8E1 appears to be 6034393. *TACOM LCMC History Office*

CHAPTER 2
M20 Armored Utility Car

As mentioned in the introduction, it was intended from the outset that the T22 (M8) serve as a basis for various other vehicle configurations. The Tank Destroyer Command requested that an armored command car and an armored personnel/cargo/ammunition carrier be developed.

This initiative was formally recommended by OCM 19347 on December 17, 1942, and approved by OCM 19431 on December 31. It was a good thing that this was approved, because as an example of the fast pace of the war effort, a letter purchase order had been issued for the vehicles on October 29, and a formal supplement to the contract issued on November 1.

However, the OCMs did formalize the designations of these derivative vehicles as follows:

Carrier, Personnel-Cargo, T20
Car, Command, Armored, T26

Also included in the Tank Destroyer request and the OCM was the "Carriage, Motor, Multiple Gun, T69," which is discussed in the next chapter.

Initially, it was planned that the command car was to retain the M8 turret, but with the gun mount removed and the opening covered with armor. The turret half roof, then planned for use, was also to be removed, and additional communications equipment installed. The armored personnel carrier would have the turret removed, as well as the roof of the fighting compartment, and raised sides were to be installed in their place.

However, upon further study, the Tank Destroyer Command agreed to a turretless command car. After some time, it was concluded that a single vehicle could fulfill both missions, and accordingly, on March 18, 1943, OCM 19993 formalized the replacement of the two contemplated vehicles with the Armored Utility Car T26.

The pilot vehicle was completed in February and underwent testing at Aberdeen Proving Ground from March 10 through 18. This went well enough that the vehicle was recommended for standardization, and the pilot was then driven to Camp Hood, Texas.

Acting on the Aberdeen recommendation, OCM 20077, of April 1, 1943, recommended standardizing the T26 as the Car, Armored, Utility, M10. This recommendation was approved on May 6. One week later, the Ordnance Committee recognized that confusion had arisen in combat units when more than one type of vehicle uses the same "M number." Since the Tank Destroyers were already employing the M10 3-inch Gun Motor Carriage, the decision was made to redesignate the M10 armored car as the Armored Utility Car M20.

Ford had meanwhile, on March 23, 1943, been contracted to produce 6,622 of the vehicles. Production of the vehicles began in Chicago on April 15, 1943. The Chicago plant would be the sole producer of the M20.

Armament of the M20 had been specified as one M2 HB .50-caliber machine gun on M49 ring mount per OCM 20680, of June 10, 1943. However, recognizing that the gun would not be needed in every role, on September 9, 1943, this specification was changed, such that the ring mount would be installed on all vehicles, but the gun itself would be separate issue as needed. On August 17, 1944, approval was given to using the M66 ring mount rather than the M49; however, this change did not enter production.

On November 30, 1944, OCM 25887 recommended the installation of a second generator on all M20s equipped with two radios. This recommendation was approved on December 21, by OCM 26140.

Production of the M20 peaked in November 1943, at 320 units.

Ultimately, on August 17, 1945, the contract was terminated, with production to cease when 3,790 M20 armored cars had been produced.

At the request of the Tank Destroyer Force, development of a command vehicle and a personnel and cargo carrier based on the Light Armored Car M8 chassis commenced in December 1942. These were designated Personnel-Cargo Carrier T20 and the Armored Command Car T26. Ultimately, both vehicles were combined into a single one, the Armored Utility Car T26, later standardized as the M20. As seen in this photo of the left side of a mockup of the T20, the vehicle lacked the turret and fighting-compartment roof and included an open-topped shield around the upper body between the drivers' compartment and the engine deck. A .50-caliber machine gun was mounted behind the front of the shield. Unpainted plywood was used for the shield on the mockup, and the body and fenders of the mockup were of painted or stained plywood. *Benson Ford Archives*

Six civilian workers are sitting sideways and face to face in the T20 mockup. The shield atop the body was fabricated from ¼-inch plywood with lumber braces. The body and chassis of the mockup may have been one that had been used in the development of the Light Armored Car M8. *Benson Ford Archives*

Several modifications were made to the shield on the T20 mockup. In this iteration, a peaked section was on top of the front of the shield, likely to protect the base of the machine gun mount. The production T20/M20 would dispense with the peaked top. *Benson Ford Archives*

As work on the mockup progressed, various methods of supporting a skate mount over the passenger compartment were tried, including this installation of a M49C ring mount. *Benson Ford Archives*

The pilot Armored Utility Car T26 was completed in February 1943 and tested at Aberdeen Proving Ground in March. It was then driven to Camp Hood, Texas, where it was photographed on May 6, 1943, during testing by the Tank Destroyer Board. The open-topped structure atop the body, referred to in technical manuals as the protection shield, is similar in design to one of the versions on the T26 mockup, but with angled plates between the sides and the front of the shield. Bolted to the rear part of the protection shield was an M49 ring mount for a .50-caliber machine gun. *National Archives*

The pilot T26 is viewed from above during evaluations by the Tank Destroyer Board. Each of the three support brackets of the M49 ring mount was secured to the protection shield by four bolts. The vehicle could carry up to seven troops or 3,000 pounds of cargo. Note the wooden-slat bench seats, the radio in the left rear of the cargo compartment, and the artillery ammunition packing tubes at the front of the compartment. *National Archives*

In a frontal view of the pilot T26 at Camp Hood in May 1943, note the early version of supports for the top hatch covers, on the sides of the drivers' compartment. Three footman loops for securing a canvas top are on the front of the protection shield. One footman loop is on each of the angled plates to the sides of the front plate of the shield. *National Archives*

The top and front hatch covers are open on the pilot T26. As was the case on the Light Armored Car M8, each front hatch had a periscope with a crash pad, and a direct-vision port with a swiveling cover. Between the front hatches is a latch assembly for securing those hatches when open. *National Archives*

In the right sponson of the pilot T26, as photographed at Camp Hood in May 1943, are a Radio Receiver BC-312-D, and, *left*, a dynamotor, for converting direct current into alternating current. These were part of the Radio Set SCR-193. *National Archives*

Several other radio sets were tested in the right sponson of the pilot Armored Utility Car T26 at Camp Hood in early May 1943. This is a Radio Set SCR-608, which, according to the descriptive label for the photo, protruded 3 inches "beyond the outside of the sponson," which presumably means it jutted 3 inches into the fighting compartment. *National Archives*

Shown here in the right sponson of the pilot T26 is a Radio Set SCR-506, which combined the Radio Receiver BC-652 and the Radio Transmitter BC-653. This set protruded 4.75 inches beyond the sponson. *National Archives*

In this instance, a Radio Set SCR-193 has been installed in the left side of the crew compartment of the pilot T26 at Camp Hood in May 1943. This set included a Radio Transmitter BC-191 (*upper left*), a Radio Receiver BC-312 (*right*), and a Dynamotor BD-77. On the rack to the lower left is another radio set. *National Archives*

The final photo of a radio installation in the pilot T26 shows a Radio Set SCR-610 in the right sponson, with the front of the set to the right. This small set was intended for short-range ground communications, up to 5 miles. *National Archives*

An early-production Armored Utility Car M20, serial number 181 and registration number 60110953, was photographed during evaluations by the Ordnance Operation, Engineering Standards Vehicle Laboratory, Detroit, Michigan, on March 24, 1944. *Patton Museum*

In a frontal view of M20 registration number 60110953, compare the production-type supports for the top hatch covers with those in the earlier photos of the pilot Armored Utility Car T26. The single footman loop on each of the small, angled plates on the sides of the protection shield were mounted horizontally, whereas the loops on these plates on the pilot T26 were welded on at an angle. This feature is also visible in subsequent photos. *Patton Museum*

M20 registration number 60110953 is viewed from the rear, with the .50-caliber machine gun and carriage positioned on the left side of the Ring Mount M49. The mudguards on the rears of the fenders of the early M20s lacked the stamped stiffeners that would be introduced later. The exhaust tailpipe opening is below the right mudguard. Note the machine gun tripod to the rear of the protection shield. *Patton Museum*

As seen from the left rear of M20 registration number 60110953, most structural details of the vehicle, with the exception of the replacement of the turret by the protection shield and ring mount, are identical to those of an early-production Light Armored Car M8. Blanket rolls are strapped to the protection shield. *Patton Museum*

Early M20s had the racks for three M1A1 antitank mines on the sponsons. An ax and a shovel are stored on brackets and secured with webbing straps atop the sponson. Footman loops for securing blanket rolls on the protection shield were limited to the rear of the support brackets of the ring mount. Other footman loops toward the bottom of the protection shield were for securing a canvas top over the shield. *Patton Museum*

A disassembled mattock is stored atop the right sponson. A single radio antenna is mounted atop the right fender; on the opposite side of the vehicle was a location for an additional antenna. Note the quick-release pintle hook protruding from the rear of the vehicle. *Patton Museum*

The general arrangement of M20 registration number 60110953 is viewed from above on March 24, 1944. Details include the clamp for securing the tow cable on the rear of the engine deck, the hole on the left fender for installing an antenna mount, two of the three flanges on the ring mount that are bolted to the support brackets, and the Rocket Launcher M1 or M1A1, "Bazooka," along with several rockets, stored on the inside front of the protection shield. *Patton Museum*

The crew compartment of the same M20 is viewed from the front, with the top hatches of the drivers' compartment open in the foreground. Visible in the compartment are two blanket rolls, ammunition boxes, three stored M1 .30-caliber carbines, a fire extinguisher, a bench/platform, a binoculars case in a holder, and a 5-gallon liquid container. *Patton Museum*

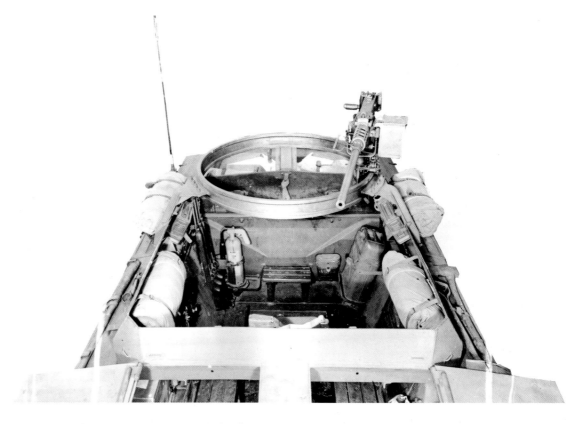

The crew compartment is viewed from the rear, with the M49 ring mount in the foreground. Note the pronounced hump in the center of the floor, to provide clearance for the drivetrain. On the right side of the compartment are three M1 carbines in brackets and, in the sponson, radio equipment. On the left side of the compartment are a 5-gallon liquid container and a storage chest. At the center front of the compartment is a folding desk for the commander, in the lowered position. Stowed at the front of the compartment are a Rocket Launcher M1 or M1A1 and 2.63-inch Rockets M6A1. *Patton Museum*

Located in the right sponson next to the troop bench are, *from left*, a Radio Transmitter BC-604 and two Radio Receivers BC-603. These were elements of the Radio Set SCR-508. The canister-shaped object to the lower left is an A-62 phantom antenna. Above the radio is a blanket roll over a canvas case containing a signal-flag set. To the far right are a hand-grenade box and a Kidde fire extinguisher. To the far left is the commander's desk, stored in the raised position. *Patton Museum*

In the left rear corner of the crew compartment of M20 registration number 60110953 are the liquid container, a hand-grenade box, and a canteen and a .30-caliber ammunition box, below which is a spare .50-caliber machine gun barrel. To the lower right are doors for the left sponson, which contains spare-parts storage. At the upper center, below the ring mount, are the locking handle for the machine gun carriage, and a flashlight stored on clips. *Patton Museum*

The drivers' compartment is viewed from the front of the crew compartment. At the center is the transmission gearshift lever. An M1 carbine is stored on each side of the compartment. To the front of the codriver's seat are clips for holding lubrication charts and manuals. Below the clips is stored a headlight assembly, below which are storage boxes for two periscopes, labeled "PROTECTOSCOPES." To the right of the steering wheel is the hand-brake lever. To the left of the steering gearbox at the bottom of the steering column is the clutch pedal; to the right of the gearbox are the brake and accelerator pedals. *Patton Museum*

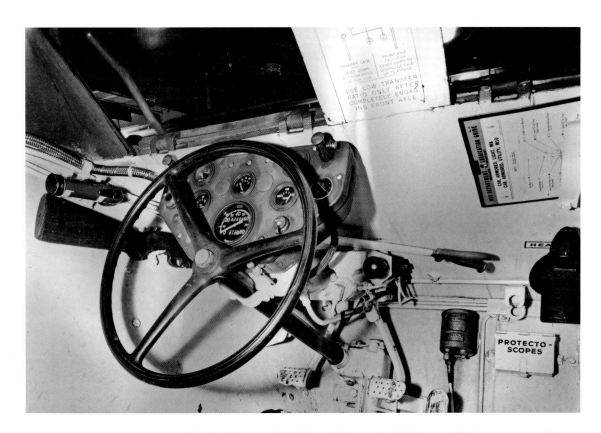

In a close-up of the front of the driver's compartment of M20 registration number 60110953, below the hand-brake lever and to the right of the instrument panel is a black knob: the priming pump. To the immediate left of the knob are the master cylinders for the clutch, *left*, and the brake, *right*. The cylinder below the handle of the hand brake is the throttle-control fluid reservoir. *Patton Museum*

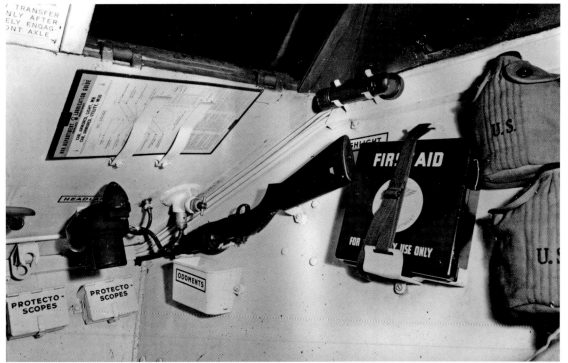

The codriver's compartment is viewed close-up. On the sidewall are two canteens, a first-aid kit, an oddments bin, an M1 carbine, and a flashlight. Above the oddments bin on the inside of the glacis is the electrical connection for the right headlight assembly, as well as a T-handle for locking the removable headlight assembly in its mount. Between that fixture and the spare headlight assembly is the electrical cable and connection for the horn. *Patton Museum*

An early Armored Utility Car M20 completed in 1943, in the collection of Paul Viens, is on display. In this lighting, the weld beads on the edges of the protection shield and the body are particularly prominent. *David Doyle*

The M20 in the Viens collection is viewed from the rear. Early M20s lacked the stamped stiffeners on the mudguards below the rears of the fenders. The engine-compartment doors are open, supported by white rods. Below the body, the muffler, rear axle, and shock absorbers are in view. *David Doyle*

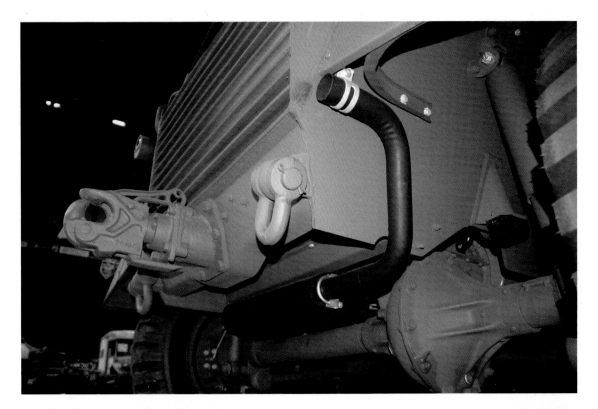

The muffler, tailpipe, and clamps are seen from a closer perspective. As built, the M20s were equipped with Gabriel direct-acting shock absorbers. Next to the shock absorber is a rear-axle snubber. Also in view are the pintle hook and the right-rear tow eye and clevis. *David Doyle*

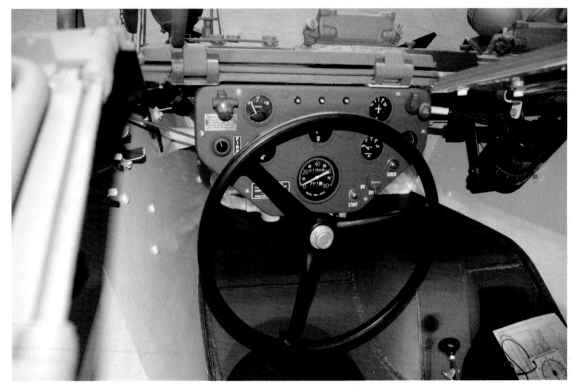

The instrument panel, steering wheel, hand-brake lever, and hinges for the front hatch cover are shown. To the right is a periscope below the codriver's front hatch cover. Note the weld beads on the floor, which is painted Olive Drab. *David Doyle*

A view into the driver's top hatch includes his and the codriver's seats, the instrument panel and steering wheel, and the transmission shift lever. Partially visible on each side of the transmission shifting lever are levers for engaging the front axle and selecting the transfer-case ratio. *David Doyle*

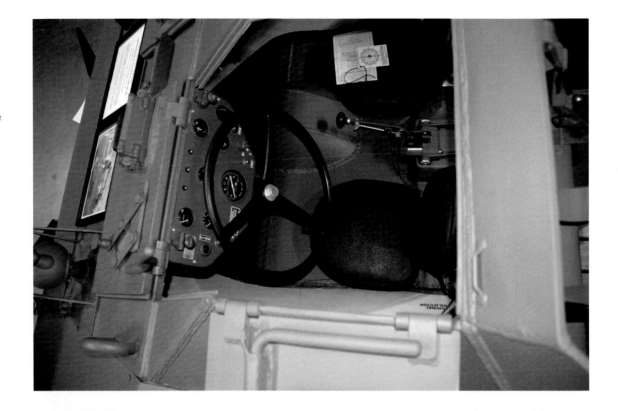

A view through the codriver's hatch of the M20 provides a close look at the flanges around the sides and rear of the hatch, for holding the front and top hatch covers when closed. Near the top of the interior of the driver's compartment, to the immediate rear of the mechanism for opening and closing the cover of the driver's-side direct-vision port, there is a small, round object. This is the control for unlatching the top hatch cover when in the open position. *David Doyle*

The rear of the crew compartment of the M20 in the Viens collection features various storage containers and brackets, labeled with decals, including grenade boxes, fire extinguisher, binoculars, water can, and spare .50-caliber machine gun barrel. *David Doyle*

A view into the left side of the engine compartment from the rear of the M20 shows the top of the radiator (*foreground*); the valve cover, spark plugs, and ignition harness (*right*); carburetor (*center background*); and the air cleaner (*left*). Cans for extra engine oil, and an oil can, are stored on the left wall of the compartment. *David Doyle*

In the right side of the engine compartment, as seen from the rear of the M20, in the foreground is the radiator filler cap. To the left are the generator, oil filter, and crankcase breather / oil-filler cap. On the right side of the compartment are, *from the foreground forward*, a white-colored shunt box, the voltage regulator (black, on a white bracket), and the battery. *David Doyle*

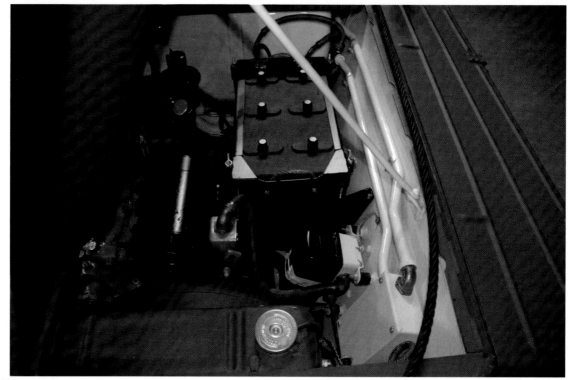

Photographed during evaluations by the Ordnance Operation, Engineering Standards Vehicle Laboratory, Detroit, on February 16, 1945, Armored Utility Car M20 with serial number 3038 exhibits a mixture of early-production features, such as the mine rack on the sponson, and later features, including the box for storing windshields, on the glacis. On the interior of the column separating the driver's and codriver's front hatches are visible a cam latch and a grab handle. The swiveling, L-shaped handles on the top-hatch covers are in the raised positions. *Patton Museum*

M20 serial number 3038 is shown with a canvas cover installed over the crew compartment during testing on February 16, 1945. The cover is secured with straps to the footman loops around the protection shield. In the preceding photo, this cover is rolled up and strapped, wraparound fashion, to the rear part of the protection shield. *Patton Museum*

Another late-production feature on M20 serial number 3038 is the stamped stiffeners on the mudguards below the rears of the fenders. However, this vehicle lacked perhaps the most prominent feature of late-production M20s: the storage boxes on the sides of the sponsons, which replaced the mine racks. *Patton Museum*

Armored Utility Car M20, serial number 3038, is viewed from the front with the drivers' hatch covers open. Note the L-shaped tabs on the front of the windshield-storage box, which are bolted to the glacis. *Patton Museum*

The Browning .50-caliber M2 HB machine gun and its carriage are swung around to the rear of the M49 ring mount in this left-side photo of M20 serial number 3038. *Patton Museum*

In this right-hand view of the same M20, under high magnification the vehicle's registration number is visible on the sponson above the recognition star: 60113810. The registration number was painted in drab blue over the Olive Drab camouflage, to reduce the visibility of the number. *Patton Museum*

M20 serial number 3038 is viewed from above, with the canvas cover installed over the crew compartment. A machine gun tripod is stored on the fuel-tank cover to the rear of the crew compartment. Two blanket rolls are strapped to the ventilation hood on each of the engine-compartment doors. There were four footman loops on each hood for this purpose. *Patton Museum*

The same M20 is seen from above without the crew-compartment cover erected, during evaluations in Detroit on February 16, 1945. That canvas cover may be seen strapped to the rear part of the protection shield. Rockets in packing tubes for the bazooka are secured to the inside of the front of the protection shield. *Patton Museum*

In a view of the driver's and codriver's compartment from the rear, the lower part of the grab handle between the forward hatches is visible at the top center, to the right of the instructional placard for the levers for the transfer-case selector and front-axle disengagement. A good view is available of the mounting brackets for the compass, below the codriver's front hatch. This compass was manufactured by Sherrill Company. *Patton Museum*

The rear of the front of the protection shield of M20 serial number 3038 is displayed, with a bazooka and inert rockets stored on it. At the center is the commander's desk, locked in the raised position. *Patton Museum*

The rear of the crew compartment is seen through the M49 ring mount, showing a stored M1 carbine, the two grenade boxes and fire extinguisher, a stored bazooka rocket, a binoculars holder, and a 5-gallon water container. Note the holders for the carbine butts on the floor toward the lower left. *Patton Museum*

The right side of the fighting compartment of the same M20 is shown in a February 14, 1945, photograph. In the sponson is an SCR-508 radio set, equipped with a rolled-up canvas cover. Below the bench next to the radio are an ammunition box and two boxes for smoke pots. To the far right, above the fire extinguisher, is the battery master switch. *Patton Museum*

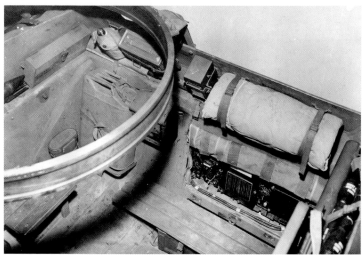

In a view of the left side of the crew compartment of M20 serial 3038, a radio set is mounted in the sponson. A rolled-up canvas cover for the radio is supplied with a zipper on each side for securing it shut when lowered. *Patton Museum*

An auxiliary generator and regulator were installed in Armored Utility Car M20s furnished with two radio sets, so that the dual sets could be operated as radio relay stations without running the engine or exhausting the battery. In July 1943, the Army procured 500 auxiliary generators for this purpose, and by early March 1944 the generators had been tested and were approved for installation in M20s above serial number 1512. According to a contemporaneous report from the chief of Ordnance, all Armored Utility Cars M20 built after November 1, 1943, came installed with brackets for the auxiliary generator. The Autolite auxiliary generator seen here on the left side of the engine compartment of an M20 is an incomplete installation, evidently for demonstration or experimental purposes. Like the stock generators, the auxiliary generators were belt driven, but the belt has not been installed on this unit. *Bill Kish collection*

An auxiliary-generator installation, complete, is shown in previously illustrated M20 serial number 3038, toward the right, near the radiator. The drive belt and electrical cable are present. The photo was taken on February 1, 1945, during evaluations by the Ordnance Operation, Engineering Standards Vehicle Laboratory, Detroit. *Patton Museum*

An Armored Utility Car M20 that was in the collection of the late Kevin Kronlund is on display. The two whip antennas are secured with cords to the brush guards. White stencils that read "TP45," for "Tire Pressure 45 [psi]," are on the fenders. This stenciling was not introduced until after World War II. *David Doyle*

The left front of the protection shield, the stored shovel and ax, and the upper part of the left sponson are depicted close-up, with details of the welds visible. A clear view of the left support of the M49 ring mount also is available. *David Doyle*

The left mine racks are carrying a full complement of M1A1 antitank mines, which are secured with a webbing strap over their tops. The outer extension of the lower rack served as a crew step. *David Doyle*

The Kronlund M20 is parked in a field next to an M1A1 heavy wrecker. This M20 has the embossed or stamped stiffeners on the mudguards to the rear of the fenders. It also has the late-type configuration of the tailpipe, which protrudes through a hole in the right mudguard. *David Doyle*

A rear view of the M20 provides clear details of the shape of the stamped stiffener on the sheet metal of the right mudguard. An armored box for a first-aid kit covers the stamped stiffener on the left mudguard, which was the mirror image of the one on the right mudguard. *David Doyle*

Details displayed in this rear view include the taillight assemblies, the rear lifting eyes, the ventilation hoods and the recessed troughs on the engine-compartment doors, and the fuel-tank cover just behind the rear of the protection shield. Each engine-compartment door has two L-shaped lock handles and a grab handle. *David Doyle*

Of particular interest in this right-front photo of the Kronlund M20 is the fact that the vehicle was fitted for carrying a storage box for detachable windshields on the glacis. Though the box is missing, three bosses for screwing on the box are visible: two are on the lower quarters of the white circle surrounding the recognition star, for fastening the front of the box, and a single boss is above the circle, for securing the rear of the box. *David Doyle*

The Kronlund M20 is viewed from the right side, showing two webbing straps attached to footman loops on the rear part of the protection shield, for securing blanket rolls. The lock hasps on the hinged covers for the fender storage compartments are secured with snap hooks on retainer chains. *David Doyle*

The right mine rack, with three M1A1 antitank mines and a webbing retainer strap, and details of the side skirts and the protection shield are displayed. *David Doyle*

The right side skirt, with its two stamped stiffeners, is depicted, along with two of the lock hasps and snap hooks for securing the covers for the fender storage compartments. The skirt hinges are of authentic format, with the leaves attached to the hull with three hex screws and lock washers, and the bottom leaves welded to the skirt. *David Doyle*

This restored, 1944-production Armored Utility Car M20 is in the collection of John Cliche. Mounting bosses for a windshield box are not present on the glacis. The rearview mirror mounted on brackets on the left side of the glacis appears to be a postwar modification. *David Doyle*

The M20 features the late-style routing for the tailpipe, through an opening in the right mudguard. Embossed stiffeners are present on the mudguards. The covers for the fender storage compartments are open. *David Doyle*

The muffler and the lower part of the taillight of the Cliche M20 are viewed from behind the right-rear tire. Note the V-shaped bracket, welded to the hull, for the tailpipe holder. The rear axle is the Ford GAA model. *David Doyle*

The covers of the storage compartments on the left fender are open, showing some of the stowed equipment inside. Note the hold-open rods and the V-shaped stiffener, fabricated from hat channels, on the inside of the closer hinged cover. *David Doyle*

The storage compartment on the left rear fender is viewed from the side with the hinged cover secured in the open position. In addition to the hat-channel stiffener inside the cover, there are two embossed stiffeners on the cover, running from front to rear. *David Doyle*

The storage compartment on the front left fender was earmarked for stowing six tire chains. The hinged cover on this compartment had a straight hat-channel stiffener on its inner side, mounted diagonally. *David Doyle*

The storage compartment on the right-rear fender is shown with the cover raised, with various items of equipment stored inside. *David Doyle*

The front-right storage compartment held a hand-type grease gun (seen here on a tool roll), a gasoline cooking outfit, a pair of asbestos mittens, and an M1939 machete. *David Doyle*

The codriver's compartment is viewed through the driver's hatch, showing the seat and safety belt and, *left to right*, the red handle of the manual brake, the compass and grab handle, a clip for storing an M1 carbine, a flashlight, first-aid kit, two stowed canteens, and binoculars. *David Doyle*

The crew compartment of the M20 that belonged to the late Kevin Kronlund is viewed from the codriver's compartment, with his seat in the foreground. Note the tunnel on the crew-compartment floor, for clearance for the drivetrain below. *David Doyle*

The right side of the Kronlund M20's crew compartment is illustrated, with the commander's folding desk to the left. At the center are the right crew bench and sponson, with an unusual hinged panel or tray mounted in the opening. A stand of three M1 carbines are in the rack to the right. *David Doyle*

A Rocket Launcher M1, as distinguished from the Rocket Launcher M1A1 by the presence of a grip to the front of the shoulder rest, is stored on the interior of the front of the protection shield in the Kronlund M20. At the lower center are the levers for the transfer case and the front-axle disengage. *David Doyle*

The right crew bench, carbines and rack, fire extinguisher, rear crew seat, and binoculars holder are shown. Note how the rear seat is on hinges attached to the rear of the compartment. In the corner of the compartment, adjacent to the fire extinguisher, are a stored flashlight and the battery master switch. *David Doyle*

Later Armored Utility Cars M20 were equipped with sponson boxes with a recessed step on the lower rear. This vehicle is furnished with these boxes, as well as a box for detachable windshields on the glacis. The ring mount remains the M49. *Benson Ford Archives*

The same late M20, observed from the left side, has blanket rolls strapped to the protection shield and the tops of the ventilation hoods on the engine-compartment doors. *Benson Ford Archives*

The box for storing detachable windshield assemblies is present on the glacis of the M20. T hooks are pinned to the towing eyes on the lower front panel of the hull. *Benson Ford Archives*

With no armored first-aid kit installed on the left mudguard, the stamped stiffeners on that mudguard as well as the one on the right mudguard are clearly visible. Welded to both of the triangular panels to each side of the radiator grille are two small, round objects, which appear to be bosses for attaching part of the planned winterization gear. These objects are not found on early M20s. *Benson Ford Archives*

An elevated view of the late-production M20 provides a vivid image of the tunnel on the floor of the crew compartment, which was necessary to allow clearance for the drivetrain. The single bracket for securing the rear of the windshield box to the glacis is in view. *Benson Ford Archives*

Armored Utility Car M20 with serial number 6627 and registration number 60131943 was photographed during testing by the Ordnance Operation, General Motors Proving Ground, on March 31, 1945. The canvas top is installed over the crew compartment, including the M49 ring mount and .50-caliber machine gun. *Patton Museum*

The crew-compartment cover, as installed on M20 registration number 60131943, is observed from the left rear. The standard cover for the crew compartment was Ordnance part number 6567438 or D67438. The number 8776 on the vehicle was that assigned by GM Proving Ground. *Patton Museum*

CHAPTER 3
Multiple Gun Motor Carriage T69 and Armored Chemical Car T30

From the earliest development of the Light Armored Car M8, there was a requirement that the chassis be suitable for installing an antiaircraft gun mount. Toward that purpose, W. L. Maxson Corporation built a powered, quadruple .50-caliber machine gun mount in an open-topped turret, which Aberdeen Proving Ground was testing on an M8 chassis by late April 1943. The vehicle was designated Multiple Gun Motor Carriage T69. The vehicle is shown here in a photo dated April 29, 1949. *TACOM LCMC History Office*

Carriage, Motor, Multiple Gun, T69

As mentioned in the previous chapter, on December 17, 1942, the Ordnance Committee recommended a multiple-gun motor carriage be developed on the basis of the M8 armored car. This initiative was approved on December 31, at which time the subject vehicle was designated Carriage, Motor, Multiple Gun, T69.

W. L. Maxson, a noted manufacturer of gun turrets, created a prototype. The turret was removed from an M8, and in its place a Maxson quadruple .50-caliber machine gun mount was installed, which was driven through Maxson's variable V-belt drive.

The turret had 360-degree traverse, variable at a rate from ¼ degree per second to 60 degrees per second. The guns could be raised to 85 degrees of elevation or depressed to −10 degrees. A Navy Mk. IX reflex sight was installed.

The pilot model arrived at Aberdeen for testing in May 1943. These tests showed that the gun mount trunnions needed strengthening, as did the sight brackets, and significant improvements needed to be made in the discarding of expended cartridges and links. Maxson made the requested changes, and the vehicle was given another firing test at Aberdeen. From there, it was tested by the Antiaircraft Artillery Board at Camp Davis, North Carolina, which compared the vehicle to the M16 and M17 half-track multiple-gun motor carriages. The board found that the T69 was inferior to the half-track vehicles in many ways, including mobility, effectiveness of fire, dispersion, and weight-carrying capacity.

Thus the board concluded that the T69 did not meet the requirements of the Antiaircraft Command. Accordingly, on March 23, 1944, Ordnance Committee canceled the project through OCM 23280.

Car, Armored, Chemical, T30

On June 3, 1943, responding to a request from the Armored Force, OCM 20610 recommended the development of a version of the M8 as a rocket launcher for use by attached Chemical Corps units, and classified this project as Secret. This recommendation was approved on June 21 by OCM 20881, and the vehicles were designated Car, Armored, Chemical, T30.

The vehicles were to be armed with ten rocket launchers. Three of the vehicles were to incorporate five rocket racks on either side of the turret, which was to have 20-degree traverse, and the racks were to have 55-degree elevation. Stowage was to be provided for fifteen additional 7-inch rockets. The other three units were to incorporate Chemical Corps equipment from prints furnished by the government.

Ford bid on developing and building the six pilot T30 chemical cars on August 28, 1943. However, little progress had been made when the strategic and tactical situations changed, eliminating the need for such vehicles. Thus, on November 18, 1943, OCM 22130 recommended the project be dropped. This recommendation was approved by OCM 22265 on December 2, 1943.

The Browning M2HB .50-caliber machine guns are at maximum elevation and traversed to the rear in this left-rear view of the T69 at Aberdeen on April 29, 1943. The mudguards have modified stiffeners of a "T" shape and also have small, recessed openings in the upper inboard corners. It is unclear what these were for, but they may have been exhaust ports for the auxiliary power unit that was part of the T69. *Patton Museum*

The turret was fabricated from .375-inch rolled homogeneous steel armor. The two bulges on the upper rear of the turret were to allow clearance for the rears of the receivers of the machine guns. The round bulges toward the front of each side of the turret provided clearance for the trunnions of the gun mount, as will become clear in a later photograph. *Patton Museum*

During firing tests of the quadruple .50-caliber machine guns of the T69 at Aberdeen on May 17, 1943, a rig has been set up to record "hop," the movement of the vehicle while the guns are fired: a situation that could result in dispersion of the shots. The rig included a marking device (pen or pencil) clamped to both sides of the rear of the vehicle and to the front right of the vehicle, and corresponding wooden stands that made contact with the marking devices. As the vehicle hopped around during firing, the marking devices recorded the hop pattern on charts tacked to the stands. Note the open covers of the gun's receivers. *Patton Museum*

The turret operator of the T69 is switching on the power for the turret drive during firing tests at Aberdeen on May 17, 1943. Note the link from the gun mount to the US Navy Mk. 9 illuminated gunsight, for tilting the sight in unison with the guns. The flexible feed chute of the left outboard machine gun is routed to an electric-assist feed unit manufactured by Bell Aircraft. An Ordnance Department report dated the same day as this photo noted that firing tests of the T69 at Aberdeen were proceeding "very well" but that there was a problem of ammunition jamming in the feed chute for the left outboard gun (i.e., the upper gun in this photo). The report assured that Maxson was working to correct the issue. *Patton Museum*

A GI is loading the ammunition boxes for the inboard machine guns of the T69 during tests at Aberdeen Proving Ground on May 22, 1943. To the rear of the soldier is what appears to be an electrical motor with an intercom control box attached to its front. *Patton Museum*

After the tests of the Multiple Gun Motor Carriage T69 at Aberdeen in April 1943, modifications were made to the turret armor and the gun mount, which are documented in the following sequence of photos. Compare them with the April–May 1943 photos of the same vehicle. In this front-right view dated August 24, 1943, the cutouts for the machine guns on the front of the armored shield have been remodeled, eliminating the curves at the bottoms of the openings. *Patton Museum*

On the same date as the preceding photo, the turret of the T69 is traversed to the rear, and the .50-caliber machine guns are at maximum elevation of 85 degrees. At full depression, the guns were at –10 degrees. Note the battered rear of the left skirt and mudguard. *Patton Museum*

Several changes are visible in this view of the modified T69 on August 24, 1943. The bulges on the upper rear of the turret have been removed, with cutouts in the armor to allow clearance for the rears of the outboard machine guns. Also, the linkage from the gun mount to the gunsight had been redesigned, and there was a new structure, the purpose of which is unclear, to the right side of that linkage. *Patton Museum*

In a photo of the T69 taken at Aberdeen Proving Ground on September 3, 1943, the turret armor has been removed, permitting a good view of the quadruple machine-gun mount. The guns were mounted on a cast cradle; trunnions on the sides of the cradle rested in bearings on fabricated supports. *Patton Museum*

General Data			
Model	**M8**	**M20**	**T69**
Weight*	14,500	12,250	17,140
Width**	100	100	100
Length***	197	197	197
Height***	90	91	85
Crew	4	6	4
Tire size	9.00-20	9.00-20	9.00-20
Maximum speed	56	55	55
Fuel capacity	54	56	56
Range	250	350	350
Electrical	12-volt negative ground	12-volt negative ground	24-volt negative ground
Transmission			
Speeds	4 forward	4 forward	4 forward
	1 reverse	1 reverse	1 reverse
Transfer speeds	2	2	2
Turning radius feet	28	28	28
Armament			
Main	37 mm	1 × .50 cal. machine guns	4 × .50 cal. machine guns
Secondary	1 × .30 cal. machine guns		
	1 × .50 cal. machine guns		

* weight unladen
** inside/outside width at tires
*** overall dimensions listed in inches

Engine Data	
Engine make/model	Hercules JXD
Number of cylinders	6
Cubic-inch displacement	320
Horsepower	110 @ 3,200
Torque	220 @ 1,150

Radio Equipment

Communications was important in the reconnaissance role, and the M8 was normally equipped with one of the following sets: (SCR-506 or SCR-193T or AN/GRC-9) or (SCR-506 or SCR-193T or SCR-608B or RC-99) or (SCR-506 or SCR-193T or AN/GRC-9 or SCR-694C and SCR-619 or SCR-610 and RC-99; or SCR-169 or SCR-610) and (RC-99).

For its role, the M20 was normally equipped with one of the following sets: (SCR-506 or SCR-694C or AN/GRC-9) and (SCR-506 or SCR-608 or SCR-510 or SCR-619 or SCR-610); or (AN/VRC-3); or (AN/VRC-3); or (AN/GRC-3,-4,-5,-6,-7, or -8) and (SCR-506).

CHAPTER 4
Field Use

Four Armored Cars M8, and an M8 or and M20 under a tarpaulin in the background, are undergoing repairs by the Motor Repair Section of the 102nd Cavalry Group at a depot in Exeter, England, on March 17, 1944. The M8 that is fully visible to the right is registration number 6032889. "CAUTION LEFT HAND DRIVE" stencils are on the turret of the closest M8 and the one whose rear is toward the camera, and on the right mudguard of registration number 6032889. *National Archives*

Late in 1943, the M8 began to reach US troops in the Mediterranean theater, but delays in production and the low war priority rating meant that the full quantities desired of these vehicles were not reaching the troops. Thus, in many units the M2 half-track was used instead of the specified M8. The vehicles also proved vulnerable to mines. Command in North Africa issued a work order for a field modification to augment the belly armor of the vehicle. This was forwarded to the European theater, which issued it as Ordnance Technical Bulletin 35 on April 28, 1944. This involved mounting a ¼-inch face-hardened armor plate to the bottom of the front compartment.

By the time of the Normandy invasion, many of the vehicles involved in that action had been so modified. They also had been fitted with M49 ring mounts as a field expedient, since the turret-mounted antiaircraft weapon had been slow to be introduced into production. As a result, most of the M8s in theater had no such armament. This modification proved particularly fortuitous, since once the vehicles began operating in France, they were found to frequently engage not armor, but infantry. In such action, the 37 mm M2 canister round as well as the antiaircraft machine gun proved especially effective.

Time proved that though the vehicles were rarely used as intended in Europe, they were nonetheless effective. They were hampered, however, by limited off-road mobility, and difficulty maneuvering in cramped urban areas.

Peak strength of the M8 in Europe was in March 1945, when 2,884 were available. Losses from June 1944 through May 1945 totaled 961, with 2,529 remaining on strength. The M20 was produced and used in more-modest numbers, with strength peaking in May 1945, with 1,445 such vehicles on hand, and losses from Normandy through that date totaling 446 of the utility cars.

Both types were used in the Pacific as well, although in much more modest numbers, since the terrain that was encountered was not at all suitable for these vehicles. The British, though originally declining the vehicles, ultimately received 496 of the M8s, and it was they who dubbed the vehicle "Greyhound." The M8 was also furnished to the Free French forces, who received 689 examples, along with 205 of the M20s. Brazil was the final Lend-Lease recipient of the M8, with that country accepting twenty of the vehicles.

The M8 and M20 were to be replaced by the M38 armored car, but no production of that vehicle was undertaken. This is what accounts for the repeated reclassification of the M8 in 1945. As a result of no newer armored cars being procured, the M8 and M20 soldiered on in US service through the Korean War. Many allied nations during the postwar era received the cars through the Military Assistance Program, which ultimately distributed about 500 of the vehicles through 1972.

In late March 1944, a row of Light Armored Cars M8 is at the front of a large collection of US Army vehicles at Camp Tidworth, Wiltshire, England. These vehicles include armored cars, half-tracks, and high-speed tractors. Spare-parts boxes on the engine decks of the M8s have the last four digits of the vehicles' registration numbers roughly painted on them. These vehicles were being stockpiled in preparation for the Allied landings in Normandy. *National Archives*

A crew of students from the US XIX Corps Ordnance Waterproofing School, at Codford, England, is driving a waterproofed Armored Utility Car M20, registration number 60110921, into a testing tank as a final examination on April 1, 1944. The canvas cover is secured over the crew compartment. Sealant material is visible on the joints of the drivers' front and top hatch covers and on the edges of the covers of the direct-vision ports. *National Archives*

Several jeeps and an M8 from the US 5th Army have paused on a street in war-ravaged Gaeta, Italy, on May 20, 1944. The nickname "NIÑA CHIQUITA" is painted in black next to the codriver's compartment, and a 5-gallon water container is stowed to each side of the 37 mm gun mantlet. An extra set of pioneer tools—a shovel, mattock handle, and ax, are on the sponson. "TD" markings for a Tank Destroyer unit are on the glacis. *National Archives*

Happy Italian citizens celebrate the arrival of the US Army alongside an M8 from a 5th Army unit on the Via Tuscolana in the outskirts of Rome on June 4, 1944. A captured German *steel helmet* is propped up on the right side of the glacis. A nickname, "ALLIES-ANT," is painted in white on the sponson. *National Archives*

A crewman of an M8 inspects the front right wheel, minus its tire, after hitting a mine outside Castiglioncello, in Tuscany, Italy, on July 13, 1944. The wheel is damaged beyond repair. On the left side of the glacis is painted "R" for Reconnaissance Company, and "35," the vehicle's number in the order of march. *National Archives*

The crew of a Light Armored Car M8 with the nickname "COLBERT" on the skirt has paused on a street in Canisy, Normandy, on July 27, 1944, to observe the effects of recent US artillery fire. The letter *S* following the registration number, 6033442, indicates that the vehicle had undergone shielding to suppress radio interference: a necessary procedure to ensure proper operation of radio equipment. *National Archives*

During a complete overhaul of a Light Armored Car M8, British civilian mechanics employed by a US Army Ordnance base at Tidworth, England, are hoisting a Hercules engine from the vehicle on July 28, 1944. In the left foreground is the assembly of the radiator and fans. The left skirt has been removed, while the right skirt is propped up in the open position. *National Archives*

A French woman in a white dress has just handed a bottle of calvados (distilled cider) to a crewman in the turret of an M8, registration number 6035050, in Le Repas, France, on August 2, 1944. Markings on the glacis of the second M8 in the column are for Headquarters Company, 25th Cavalry Reconnaissance Squadron (Mechanized), 4th Armored Division. *National Archives*

Gunners of an M8 nicknamed "AUSTIN," *foreground*, and several half-tracks from Company A, 23rd Infantry Regiment, 7th Armored Division, are bringing their weapons to bear on German troops who are trying to outflank them on the right near Épernay, along the Marne River northeast of Paris, on August 27, 1944. This M8 has an M1919A4 .30-caliber machine gun on a nonfolding pintle mount on the rear of the turret. Another M8, with the fenders removed, is in the right background. The stencil on the front fender gives the recommended tire pressures: 60 psi on the front tires, and 50 on the rear. *National Archives*

With the help of a boom mounted on the front of a ¾-ton truck, members of Company C of an unnamed maintenance company and armored division are replacing the front axle of an M8, a few miles behind the front lines near Le Teilleul, Normandy, on August 16, 1944. Four jacks are supporting the front end of the armored car, and both front fenders have been removed to facilitate the procedure. Note the original front axle lying atop the drivers' compartment. *National Archives*

With snipers and German armor active in the area, the crews of an M8 and a half-track from the 2nd Platoon, C Troop, 113th Cavalry, are proceeding slowly and cautiously as they approach the Belgian-Dutch border on September 8, 1944. Both front fenders have been removed from the M8, and a storage rack that evidently was fabricated in the field is on the right sponson. *National Archives*

The Free French Army were users of the Armored Car M8, and this photograph documents the meeting of the occupants of M8s operated by Free French from the US 7th Army, *left*, and US Army troops from the US 3rd Army at Atun, France, on September 13, 1944. The Free French vehicle bears the nickname "Champs Elysées." The US M8 (registration number 6035010) and crew were with Combat Command B, 6th Armored Division. On the American M8, three ammunition boxes are stowed on the upper part of the mine rack, while a storage box is attached to the lower rack. *National Archives*

Although the vast majority of M8s saw service in the European and Mediterranean theaters, some examples operated in the Pacific during the last year of World War II. This M8 equipped with tire chains was photographed on Leyte, in the Philippine Islands, on October 22, 1944, as its crew kept a watch on Japanese snipers on Lebrenan Hill in the background. The only visible markings are "US ARMY" stenciled in white on the sponson and the left mudguard. *National Archives*

An Armored Utility Car M20 with no visible unit markings has paused on a street in Luxembourg City on November 11, 1944. In the right side of the crew compartment, wearing the beret, is Prince Felix of Luxembourg, who is greeting some of his subjects during his visit to the command post of the 83rd Infantry Division. *National Archives*

Three Light Armored Cars M8, a jeep, and a Light Tank M5, part of a Free French unit, are parked in Brouville, northeastern France, on Novembër 17, 1944. All three M8s have the skirts removed, and the nearest one also has the front fender removed. Tire chains are on the front and the rear tires of this vehicle, but not on the center tire. *National Archives*

A Light Armored Car M8 from the 92nd Cavalry Reconnaissance Squadron, 12th Armored Division, advances along a dusty street in a village in the Sarre-Union district of northeastern France on December 26, 1944. A ring mount with a .50-caliber machine gun is on the turret, and tire chains are draped from the rear of the hull. *National Archives*

A whitewash-camouflaged M8, followed by an M8 in its regular Olive Drab camouflage, are on a patrol in northwestern Europe on January 14, 1945. The vehicles are marked for the 2nd Cavalry Regiment, US 3rd Army. When the M8 was whitewashed, the painters took care not to cover the recognition stars and surrounding Olive Drab paint. The .50-caliber machine gun on the turret of this vehicle is on a nonfolding pintle mount on an unusual, improvised bracket on the turret roof. *National Archives*

Three members of Headquarters Company, 807th Tank Destroyer Battalion, 95th Division, are taking advantage of a shop or garage near Saarlautern, Germany, to apply a coat of whitewash winter camouflage to an Armored Utility Car M20, on January 13, 1945. The sergeant on the left is using a small paintbrush, while the one on the right is using an applicator, possibly a sponge on a long handle. Even the wheels and the sides of the tires have received whitewash. Note the storage racks on the sides of the crew compartment, a local field modification. *National Archives*

The Wehrmacht made a practice of impressing captured vehicles into its service, and such was the case with this M8, manned by a panzer crew. The Balkenkreuz recognition cross on the turret exhibits numerous runs in the white paint. Vegetation was draped over the hull and turret for camouflage, and a jerry can is in a bracket on the mudguard on the rear of the vehicle. *Patton Museum*

After capturing this M8, the Germans installed a triple MG151/20 drilling cannon mount in the turret. This combination gun mount was the same type employed in the Sd.Kfz. 251/21. The Germans effected the conversion by removing the 37 mm gun and mount, welding a steel plate over the former gun opening in the turret, and removing the semicircular roof and welding it inside the turret to form a shelf on which the MG151/20 drilling was mounted. These guns were installed so as to extend over the rear of the turret. When Army Ordnance photographed the vehicle after it was recaptured toward the end of the war, two of the three cannon barrels were not installed. *National Archives*

A Light Armored Car M8, registration number 6033224, from D Troop, US 42nd Constabulary Squadron, has paused along a road outside Grafenwöhr, West Germany, during Exercise Delay, a US 1st Infantry Division operation, on May 26, 1948. The fenders have been removed from the vehicle, and two stripes have been painted around the hull. On the glacis, the turret, and the unit markings on the bow are the insignia of the US Constabulary: a letter *C* with a lightning bolt over it. *National Archives*

Two M8s from D Troop, 16th Special Constabulary Squadron, have stopped during a patrol in the western part of Berlin on June 25, 1948. The vehicle on the left has a marking, "BERL," on the front right of the glacis, possibly standing for Berlin, while the other M8 has "OMGUS" marked in the same area, standing for Office of Military Government, United States. On the glacis of each vehicle is a round placard with the constabulary's insignia. To the rear is a Soviet war memorial featuring an IS-2 heavy tank. *National Archives*

Members of an M8 crew from the 14th Constabulary Squadron are performing bivouac guard duty for the 1st Division during Exercise Prime, at Grafenwöhr, West Germany, on August 5, 1948. The vehicle bears registration number 6035580. The original caption for the photo states that this vehicle was with the 1st Reconnaissance Company, but the letter *C* on the right mudguard represents C Troop. *National Archives*

Vehicles parked in the storage area of the 106th Ordnance Heavy Maintenance Company, 32nd Ordnance Battalion, 2nd US Logistics Command, at Pusan, South Korea, on June 6, 1952, include three Armored Utility Cars M20 in the right foreground. The registration number of the nearest M20 is visible: 60112242. *National Archives*

M8 light armored cars saw some service with the army of the Republic of Vietnam. The vehicle shown here is being manned by soldiers who were part of an attempted military coup on September 13, 1964. A spare tire has been stored on the radiator grille, and a holder for a 5-gallon liquid container is on the left mudguard. An armored shield has been fitted over the .50-caliber machine gun on the turret.
National Archives